Weather Around You
Wind

Anita Ganeri

HODDER
Wayland

an imprint of Hodder Children's Books

Weather Around You
Rain • Snow • Sunshine • Wind

Weather Around You – Wind

Commissioning Editor: Vicky Brooker   Book Editor: Katie Sergeant
Book Designer: Jane Hawkins   Picture Research: Katie Sergeant
Cover Design: Hodder Children's Books

British Library Cataloguing in Publication Data
Ganeri, Anita, 1961-
    Wind. - (Weather around you)
    1. Winds - Juvenile literature
    I.Title
    551.5'18

ISBN 075024562X

Printed and bound in China

Hodder Children's Books
A division of Hodder Headline Limited
338 Euston Road, London NW1 3BH

Cover: A Dutch windmill.

Picture Acknowledgements
The publisher would like to thank the following for permission to reproduce their pictures: Alamy 6 (Catherine Dianich Gruver); Associated Press 13 (Ron Heflin), 15 (Gregory Bull), 16 (J. Pat Carter); Corbis *Contents*, 22, 23 and 24 (Royalty-Free), 4 (Roger Ressmeyer), 5 (Francoise de Mulder), 7 (Carl & Ann Purcell), 8 (C/B Productions), *Title page* and 9 (Royalty-Free), 10 (Aaron Horowitz), 17 (Jim McDonald), 18 (ML Sinibaldi), 19 (Owaki – Kulla), 20 (Sharon Green); Getty 11 (Stone/ Alan R Moller), 14 (The Image Bank/ A. T. Willett); Robert Harding 21; Topham/ ImageWorks 12 (David M. Jennings); zefa *Cover* (K. Hackenberg).

Contents

Words in **bold** can be found in the glossary on page 23.

A windy day

You cannot see the wind. But you can feel it on your face and see how it blows the sea into **waves**. It is fun to fly a kite on a windy day.

But the wind can make life hard for people. In the desert, strong winds blow dust and sand about. It is hard to see and breathe.

What is wind?

Wind is simply air. You feel the wind blowing because of the way air moves. When air is warm, it gets lighter. It rises up into the sky.

When air is cool, it gets heavy. It sinks down to the ground. It fills the space the warm air has left behind. This is what makes the wind blow.

Breezes and gales

Sometimes the wind blows gently. A gentle wind is called a **breeze**. It makes the leaves rustle on the trees. It makes flags flap and flutter.

Sometimes the wind blows very hard. A strong wind is called a **gale**. It makes the trees bend and sway. It is hard to walk in a strong wind.

Whirling winds

The strongest winds happen in a **tornado**.
A tornado is a spinning twist of wind. It hangs
down from a huge, dark **thundercloud**.

A tornado is dangerous
if it touches the ground.
It speeds along the
ground very fast. It
sucks up anything
in its way.

Tornado damage

In a **tornado**, the wind is very fierce. It can pick up cars and trains and throw them into the air. It can also pick up people.

People cannot stop tornadoes. But they can tell if a tornado is coming. Then they can go to a shelter where they are safe.

Spinning winds

You also get strong winds in a **hurricane**. A hurricane is like a giant wheel of wind, clouds and rain. Hurricanes start over warm seas.

Watch out when a hurricane reaches
land. The strong wind smashes buildings
and pulls up trees. The wind whips up the
sea which floods on to the land.

Living with hurricanes

Weather forecasters can see if a **hurricane** is coming. They warn people to stay indoors or to go to a hurricane shelter. It is too windy and dangerous to go outside.

People try to make their houses safe. They fix strong wooden boards to their windows and doors. This stops flying objects and the wind from smashing the glass.

Wind power

The wind can be dangerous but it is also useful.
Look at this old windmill. The wind turns the
sails round. This works a machine inside the
windmill. It grinds wheat to make flour.

Today, modern windmills like
these are used to make electricity.
They are built on a windy hillside.
A group of these windmills
is called a **wind farm**.

19

Sports in wind

Sailors use the power of the wind to push their boats along. These boats have large **sails**. They can move to catch as much wind as possible.

These men are **windsurfing**. They stand on a board and let the wind push the sail along. They have to be careful to keep their balance.

Wind fact file

- The windiest place in the world is Commonwealth Bay in Antarctica. Here **gales** blow at staggering speeds of 320 kilometres an hour.

- The strongest winds on Earth are found in the centre of **tornadoes**. Weather experts think they can blow at up to 480 kilometres an hour. But they are difficult to measure because they smash measuring instruments to pieces.

- **Hurricanes** are given names, such as Andrew, Betsy and Carlos. Each year, their names go in alphabetical order and in order of boy, then girl.

- The Ancient Greeks thought the winds were made by the breath of the gods. They had eight wind gods, one for each direction the wind can blow from. These are North, South, East, West, North-East, North-West, South-East and South-West.

Glossary

breeze A gentle wind.

gale A strong wind.

hurricane A giant, spinning wheel of wind, clouds and rain.

sails 1. The wooden or metal blades on the outside of a windmill. The wind blows them and makes them go round. 2. The cloth sails on a sailing boat.

thundercloud A large, dark cloud which brings thunderstorms and rain.

tornado A spinning twist of very strong wind.

waves Ripples in the sea, caused by the wind blowing across the surface of the water.

weather forecasters People who study the weather and tell you what the weather will be like.

wind farm A group of modern windmills, used for making electricity.

windsurfing Sliding across the sea on a board, pushed by a sail.

23

Index